$6.95
0599

circuitry of veins

circuitry of veins

Sylvia Legris

TURNSTONE PRESS

Copyright © 1996 Sylvia Legris

Turnstone Press
607-100 Arthur Street
Winnipeg, Manitoba
Canada R3B 1H3

All rights reserved. No part of this book may be reproduced or transmitted in any form or by any means—graphic, electronic or mechanical—without prior written permission of the publisher. Any request to photocopy any part of this book shall be directed in writing to the Canadian Copyright Licensing Agency, Toronto.

Turnstone Press gratefully acknowledges the assistance of the Canada Council and the Manitoba Arts Council.

Some of these poems have appeared in the following: *Contemporary Verse 2, Canadian Woman Studies, Prairie Fire, Other Voices, The New Quarterly, Grain, Room of One's Own, Event, NeWest Review, Border Crossings, bite to eat place: An anthology of food poetry and poetic prose* (Redwood Coast Press), in the chapbook *pathological lies (and other disorders)* (Moonprint Press), and have been broadcast on WTN's *Writing on the Wall.*

Cover artwork: *La Bête* by Lorène Bourgeois, 1987. Monotype on paper, 7.5 ft. x 6 ft. Collection of Jana Levitt and Dean Goodman.

Design: Manuela Dias

This book was printed and bound in Canada by Hignell Printing Limited for Turnstone Press.

Canadian Catloguing in Publication Data

Legris, Sylvia

Circuitry of veins

Poems.
ISBN 0-88801-207-1

I. Title.

PS8573.E46175C57 1996   C811'.54   C96-9200439
PR9199.3.L375C57 1996

bare
hug:

all bone
—squeeze too hard
she'll break

contents

radiating effects
    radiating effects   /3
    bi lateral   /12

hungergraphs
    i heard once of a woman   /17
    she refuses to eat   /18
    where is it i can begin   /19
    most nights i can't   /20
    sometimes i dream   /21
    he edited strangers'   /23
    i feel like i'm in a dream   /26
    the clinic walls   /27
    you meet someone on the street   /28
    i have a copy of   /29
    quartet of banana desserts   /30
    this is a woman who cannot   /32
    the first time you eat   /33

sorting through documents
    maternal: ma(e)ternal   /37
    mum   /39
    sorting through documents   /40
    my mother's hands   /44
    fallout   /45
    ghost glowing   /46
    1925, howard street   /47
    birthmark   /48
    a margin of yellow   /49
    unburying ruth's ashes   /50
    as for the living?   /52

jokes at breakfast
    toetag #1   /55
    toetag #2   /56
    toetag #3   /57
    toetag #4   /58
    deep snow   /59
    insect clocks: one   /60
    insect clocks: two   /61
    letter to a pig   /62
    insect clocks: three   /63
    insect clocks: four   /64
    dog day   /65
    toetag #5   /66

empty screen (78 lbs)
    pornographies   /69
    perfect pitch   /78

notes   /81

acknowledgments

Thank you to all those who have offered encouragement at various points along the way.

Thank you in particular to Jeffrey Keller for his unwavering friendship, to Di Brandt, in whose class this all started, for her continuing support, and, *especially*, to my mentor and friend Betsy Warland, who really worked with me to pull this collection together, for her constant faith, wisdom, and insight.

Thank you also to the Canada Council Explorations Program, the Saskatchewan Arts Board, and the Manitoba Arts Council for financial assistance that allowed me to write, to the Sage Hill Writing Experience and the Banff Centre for the Arts for context and contact (ELK!), and to Lorène Bourgeois for her evocative La Bête on the cover.

And, of course, many many thank yous to Jamie Hutchison, Manuela Dias, and Christine Dulat at Turnstone for turning the manuscript into a Book.

radiating effects

I tell you
we live in constant
danger
under the sun

—Dorothy Livesay

radiating effects

the woman in the photograph has thick black hair,
heavy thighs, bare legs   posts
in the sand.

she remembers the occasion—one july camping
at lake manitoba. the man behind the camera
kneels on a rubber air mattress,
his lens burns circles in her skin
(he thought she was attractive then).

she wears cat-eyed glasses, a band holding
her hair off her forehead, a man's shirt
with the sleeves rolled up over her bathing suit.

back then she didn't worry
about the sun

                                                            [ontology

                                      oncology]

three days before the biopsy
she plants
two begonia bulbs in a peeling windowbox
where the sun is
most intense

*radiation may be administered
in the form of gamma rays or x-rays*

this   is simulation   this is

only a test:

when she lies under the simulator she
thinks of movies peter sellers *how i learned to love
the bomb dr strangelove*   this is only a test
like flight
simulation her oncologist jokes   dr strangelove (she thinks
he thinks he's attractive)

she remembers *the effect of gamma rays on
man-in-the-moon marigolds*   can't remember the story
only how beautiful joanne woodward was her daughters'
blossoming
radiance

this is

treatment

---

field

the oncologist

marks her skin

with indelible ink   the coldness

         adept

         fingers

         (she feels like a

                 museum specimen
                 an insect praying)

he inscribes a cross

along her torso

carbolfuchsin[1]

car–bo–fyu–shun

(she heard him
                    the first time)

---

[1] purple dye   dying easter eggs thin tracings of candlewax layers of pattern colour   yellow orange red blue fuchsia   her grandmother peeling beets elbows bleeding

LINAC   *LIN-AC*

(step on a crack
break your mother's ____)

**linear
acceleration**   time
sped up

her second son suspends two fluorescent grow-lamps
over the plant box   unnecessary he complains

her begonias flourish under the extra light and
she names them
little boy
and *fat man*

linear acceleration:

she holds up negatives to the kitchen light
—2 & 1/4 inch square x-rays

she remembers her x-husband's rolliflex
click   the viewfinder flipping up
twin lens intrusive eyes

she has boxes and boxes
thousands of negatives catalogued in
stiff   tissue paper (cracks
                    when flexed
                    like scorched skin)

                        a crick in her neck

several weeks into treatment
she can barely see
mapped out sections of her body
skin cracked   like tundra

                  (she'd always wanted to go
                     up north   dreamed for years of isolation

                  days
                        of darkness   children tucked

                                          out of the way)

beads of salt water
seep
from her broken skin[2]

                  body weeps[3]

---

2   as a girl she had eczema same beads of moisture inside fingers nape of neck backs of knees   she was beautiful then   her mother used to say she had a forehead like a man's a boxcar ribcage no one   would ever love her

3   [memories]

a roof hangs directly below her bedroom window. on sunny days
she sits outside, feet dangling over eaves, fingers
tracing brittle edges of shingles.[4]

on bright mornings she imagines the asphalt shingles melting
to her body's contours. sometimes mistakes the smell
of hot tar for the unfamiliar smell of her body.

she worries about longterm effects of
ultraviolet rays, spores taking root under eyes, teeth,
resilience of plants over a lifetime.

---

[4] one spring her son sprinkles carrot seeds over the eavestroughs   hadn't been cleaned for years better than mulch he said   she's never seen carrots so short   never tasted carrots so sweet

in the aftershock
she remembers

her dying grandmother
telling her:

> "There is an old saying
> that when some die, the left hand stays warm.
> They are the ones who come back when you need
> them."

in the middle of the night she types

grandmother

on the old black remington:

the mysterious box of papers on the top shelf of the kitchen
    cupboard
she looked at only on important days sundays or when aunt
    florence died
her dream about the angel of death he came to her dressed
    in black
she was hanging out clothes in the wind   her lace dress
    best pearls cheeks
rouged in a way she would have hated she slept in the
    economy coffin

sound   of her voice: "the cemetery
                    is the emptiest place in the world" [5]

---

[5] these memories   are not footnotes

bi lateral

both   sides

biopsy: procedure involving removal of a small amount of body tissue for microscopic analysis

           she'd do anything to disappear make her body smaller she remembers an image in a film: carpenter planing thighs of mannequins   wood shavings cover storage room floor with spirals of skin   *epi-*

dermis   (she has a hole scooped out the side of her neck big as a golfball

           she examines every inch of her body in the full-length mirror *(microscopic analysis)* would do anything to lose weight

doesn't know
how she got so thin

Lymphoma: type of cancer that begins in an altered lymphocyte. There are two broad categories of lymphomas: Hodgkin's disease and non-Hodgkin's lymphoma . . .

           sometimes wishes she'd get cancer so she could lose enough weight

. . . both respond favourably
to radiation

                                        she feels huge in bright light
                                        shopping malls open streets
                                        feels naked
                                        under the sun

she wears sunglasses
in the dark

hungergraphs

*Language is filled
with words for deprivation.*

—Susan Griffin

❖

i heard once of a woman so thin she could balance
an *O.E.D.* on the points of her pelvic bones
and still leave room to fit a substantial paperback:
the alexandria quartet or the *joy
of cooking*.

✣

                                          she *refuses* to eat

can't eat

21 years old
5 feet 5 inches tall
weigh 72 pounds

                                          the problem with this subject
                                          one of control

never felt so
out of control

when i came to the ward
they inserted a tube
through a hole in my left arm
monitor my every movement

                                          behaviour modification
                                          is always administered in a caring
canvas restraints   therapeutic manner
at my shoulders and feet

                                          still
                                          she remains uncooperative
treat me
like i don't exist
only see
what i won't eat

                                          she refuses to eat

❖

where is it i can begin to remember? thinness so conspicuous you can circle two fingers around each pencil of rib, around the thickest part of arm, the space below the knee. all those mornings standing bone-naked before the full-length mirror, strumming my fingers up and down my cold body. each bone sounding a different note. every inch of flesh taut
as a drum.

❖

most nights i can't sleep for the racket. it's like living
in a sweatshop, walls so transparent they vibrate
with machinery, tireless scrape of bone against socket,
every organ pumping, every hinge creaking
out of habit. i lie in bed buzzing with the hum
of refrigerator, whirring tangle of wiring
behind walls, circuitry of veins crackling beneath skin.
i count out time by strips of headlight
disappearing across the ceiling, discordant movement
intestines and stomach.

❖

sometimes i dream i'm a whittler. a girl lost
in a forest. branches sticks twigs everywhere.
piled like bones.
i dream of carving:
watermelon into perfect pink balls. kitchen linoleum
into geometric patterns—X X X X X. my arms,
skinny birch limbs, into blunt potato cuts: happy faces
with fat grins, full bellies. can't you just see it,
the pictures i can make? can't you imagine
crimson print on linen curtains, drizzles and
dribbles of cadmium red on white carpet?
action painting.

        hmmm . . .

        action.

        look around. just

        look around.

i'm standing in the middle of my apartment, blinds down,
every light but one burnt out. i have a big fluorescent calendar
on the wall above the tv, numbers three inches high,
but still i can't keep track of the date half the time.

my father says i do this for attention.

like i enjoy throwing up after every fucking meal like i
enjoy feeling like some sort of freak like i enjoy feeling

        nothing.

i can't describe the numbness. everything tingles with
insects, live wires. my gums are peeling from my teeth.
my esophagus is raw. but most of the time i feel

                nothing.

and then
i have these dreams
of sharp objects, narrow edges, near misses.
colours so vivid. everything red and white red
against white. red against white.
contrast
so stark.

not that i intend to hurt myself i just
never feel real want to feel so badly
feel

                anything.

but this skin,
it's so thin it doesn't take long
to hit bone.

how deep do i have to dig?

how little a dead person bleeds.

❖

he edited strangers' lives
other people's stories
of crime, violence, abuse
tales of upstanding gentlemen
beating wives and raping children
pinstripes strutting
cocks swaggering:
these things
were news
he corrected for typos
revised for clarity
accuracy   *truthfulness*
    even as a child she felt
the power of language the pain
inflicted with carefully placed words
(blood sharp objects
pens and pencils draw)
his job was to rearrange
body parts after an accident
remove the ugliest bits
line up the rest neatly
he was good at it
never missed a day
    for years she believed
those holes in her
were self-inflicted
he called her
illiterate yelled because
she held her pen the wrong way
said she'd never amount
to anything

she tried
not to be like him
was afraid
of her desire
to black out
white spaces
the one thing
she needed
unclean
    she could never understand
why she was equally attracted
to venus pencils
and x-acto knives
her biggest mistake
believing him a writer

he told her not long ago
how much he hated
that job   trapped
by security   benefits
promises   promotion
escape
yet every day
after his graveyard shift
he dragged his work home
clenched between fat inkstained fingers
that smudged   dirtied
everything they touched
made her fear
the weight of print
smearing her skin
    he showed her
writing as elimination

taught her how
to blot out
herself
erase things
he said never happened
she wanted to disappear
make herself thin
as a crack in the wall

❖

i feel like i'm in a dream. hands reaching out in all directions, fingers pinching grapes, fondling cantaloupe. an over-dressed old man blows his nose into a grey hanky, his free hand roaming a graveyard of wet cherries. all the times i've eaten fruit without washing it—my stomach shifts position.

the clinic walls are ice-cap blue. outside the painted-shut windows, fahrenheit and celsius are indistinguishable. despite the complimentary cups of coffee with edible-oil whitener, despite the reproductions of group of seven paintings, despite the too friendly too thin receptionist, the atmosphere here is colder than minus forty.

each week the therapist charts my height and weight in a black accounting ledger. my naked shoulder-blades cut against the crucifix of the doctor's scale. i'm not allowed to see the figures she enters, information reserved for people of significance—weight to throw around. all she'll tell me is if my weight's gone up or down. up, a measure of progress. down, of resistance.

when i gain weight the therapist praises me, makes me feel almost human. if i lose she scolds me like a child, or a dog. the weeks my weight drops she threatens to hospitalize me, force-feeding the necessary treatment for someone who refuses to understand the consequences of her own behaviour. who doesn't obey the rules.

the therapist calls it modification. her aim, she assures me, not to make me fat, but normal. she thinks of herself as a modifier: her existence qualifies mine.

❖

you meet someone on the street as thin as you, maybe thinner.
not a sliver of word passes between you.
there's a common language among the starving: incisor marks
on the backs of hands. swollen parotid glands.
silent   recognition

i have a copy of the *new york times cookbook*
my sister ordered from the book-of-the-month club
when i was 11

i've read it so many times the cover's fallen off
every page of "puddings, custards, other desserts"
stained with coffee

              (my brother

gave me the *joy of cooking* one christmas
blueprints of cows pigs meat-cut diagrams
only an architect could follow)

i like *new york times's* glossy colour photos:

    clambake by the sea complete with watermelon and beer

    roast suckling pig on a bed of parsley

    spiral bread with herbs

at night i lie in bed
buried under my cookbooks
dream about seaside   pig   turning   on spit
watermelon   beer over cracked ice

❖

quartet
of banana desserts:

bananas caribbean
banana souffles
ambrosia cake (symmetrical garnish of tangerine wedges, banana slices)
tea bread (spread with sweet butter)

when i was 13 went on my first diet
the doctor told me to avoid bananas
all starch she said

at safeway i peel blue chiquita stickers
off bananas
walk around with
chiquita sticker eyelids   bat my lashes—amazing
what people don't notice
even when i smile

                                                            amazing

what people won't see:

        a young woman works behind a bakery counter
        serving poppyseed creamcheese apple danish
        cherry blueberry rhubarb–strawberry lemon meringue pie
        12 varieties of cookies:
        shortbread crispsugar
        chocolatechip pinwheel oatmealraisin walnut spice
        hamentashen brownies fruitbars maplecream
        chocolatemacaroons and   ginger
                                                  snaps

        all day customers comment
        on her weight
                        how lucky

        toothpick arms shoulder-blades jutting out of
        her shirt

        legs thin
        as baguettes

✥

this is a woman who cannot recognise herself
in mirrors or photographs or even in the contorted
fleshpink reflection, the narrow plasticine lips,
the gaping amphibious eyes that stare back at her
from the toaster she keeps dusted like a trophy on
the white melamine table where she eats her breakfast.
etched into the shapely stainless steel curves,
forty-year-old letters fluid like ribbons:
canadian beauty. if she sits in just the right way,
positions the toaster just so, she can see the silver
letters flickering on flickering off, a neon sign
burning insensibly like mercury across her forehead.
enticing. seductive. aroma of steaming coffee, fresh
berry pie at the end of a dry highway.

the first time you eat
after not eating for years
you remember every detail:

breakfast   august 16

shell of the soft-boiled egg brown
pinkish-brown and rough
like wallpaper we'd pick off
in layers from our attic walls
each successive layer revealing
another pattern
an old personality

                my sister neatly cuts away the top of the egg
            exposing white jello-y flesh

i delve into the yolk
creamy yellow   colour
of pollen
trim rectangular strips
of toast   sagging
real salted butter
stings when it touches
my cracked mouth

                my sister fills a glossy cup
            with fresh steaming liquid

for years black and acid
beating against walls
coffee
colour of caramel
luscious and smooth
whitened and sweetened

realness of cream and sugar
beige earthenware mug
warm and soothing   cradled
against me
aroma hot   intoxicating
nourishes
my memory
long starved:

sorting through documents

*Of all my dead it's you
who come to me unfinished.*

—Adrienne Rich

maternal: ma(e)ternal

problem:

to construct a mother
from bits and pieces
name here, date there, not enough
to fill a picture: an incomplete
formation
        incomplete

        question: does a mother die
        when her body dies?

        a woman lies in bed,
        right arm bent over her eyes
        against the light

        sometimes catches herself
        in the mirror
        head held at a certain angle
        lower lip curled under her teeth

        familiar poses

                (genetic memory)

information:

my only knowledge of her relatives
comes through memories she told me
even these i remember in-

-completely:

she was born on sunnyside. had one brother, five years older who some days would walk her to school and other days pretend he didn't know her. her father was a musician, a music teacher. he left when she was eight. sometimes in the middle of the night her grandmother would hear the piano mournfully playing by itself and on the mornings following her father would turn up out of nowhere. briefly. she was embarrassed and made fun of: she was fat, ate lunches other kids laughed at (leftover stew sandwiches, lumps of potato and turnip squeezing out sides). once she wet her pants in school and had to spend the rest of the morning sitting on the radiator to dry, pee steam escaping, filling the air with laughter. she longed for her father who eventually stopped coming. she longed for her grandmother, who took care of them, to love her. she longed for her mother who lingered with cancer for years to die.

my mother's memories go

something like that

mum

when we were growing up you'd tell us how you were
the only one living from your side of the family.
you had us i thought, didn't that count?

i remember your distracted fingers cleaning crusted
ketchup off blue carpet, wringing spilled milk from
stinky dishcloths, dabbing barely workable acrylic
paint onto re-used canvas. all those years

darning transparent socks pulled tight over burnt-out
lightbulbs, filling pyrex with elbow macaroni, half
pound of hamburger stretched to

those dragged-out afternoons dying into evening,
blankets stapled across your bedroom window,
daylight pouring down walls   cracks seeping
depression

sorting through documents

i finger your death certificate
as i would an expensive piece of jewelry
carefully, anxiously
feelings and
breathing uncertain.
the hardest part
isn't the officialness, that this is it
and nothing will ever be inscribed with your name again
but it's digging this document
from the bottom of an old *nike* box
pressed flat
like a pinned-down moth
or one of those shrink-wrapped shirts
arms clasped tight at the chest
like a saint
or a mummy
hugging the air out of herself.
to get to this point
i have to sift through all your letters
all those ones you tore in half
but didn't throw away,
through piles of family photographs i can't even recognise
faces and bodies cut out
here and there
in fits of anger.

why did you do this?

even the photo of your grandmother ripped
  (you were closer to her than anyone)
                                      diagonally
through her middle
soft hands and arms severed
from her lace shoulders.

was she alive when you did this?

i've pieced the halves together
but the edges, sutured
like tattered flesh,
no longer fit.

* * *

i remember the day you died;
it was august and muggy
everything felt sick
washed-out with an intense brightness
you would have hated.
what an irony
to be pronounced dead on arrival.

i knew you'd never even arrived
before
or after.

my last image of you
your head grey and drained
awkwardly arched back against the hospital stretcher
jaw slack with relief
dentureless mouth partly open.

you would have died of embarrassment.

i touched you
your skin felt cool and bloated
puffed up like a balloon half-filled with water.
if i'd had a pin
i'd have poked you to see
if you'd deflate.

i wanted to shake you

make sure you weren't only sleeping
or pretending.
i lifted the rigid bleached sheet
i don't know why, maybe to check that you were intact

not that i would have known.

your breasts, after six children, a life
of waiting, lay flat, sullen
dead in their own right.
the flesh around your heart
where the paramedics had
pounded
pounded
pounded
tried to beat you
back to life
was bruised, bloodied

you had an odd sweet odour
slightly mildewy, slightly spicy

how death smells

                      * * *

for a long time
i tried to recapture that smell as part of you
not just the sour stench of paper bag
handed to me by a starch-faced attendant.

how does it feel
to have the last clothes you ever wore
stuffed like someone's garbage
into an IGA bag?
you didn't even shop there.

i kept that bag
in a corner of the hall for weeks
sometimes sorting through the sodden material
as if in a dream
burying my face in the cold fabric
inhaling colours through shut eyes:
your ugly red and orange poppied shirt
(the one i'd made fun of) sliced
in urgency like a registered letter
like a chicken split
in two
your navy polyester pants
static-charged with dog hair and lint
damp, urine-stained.

you would have been glad
you weren't alive to realize
you'd lost control
peed yourself like a child.

at the bottom of the bag
i found your university ring.
after your divorce
you wore this cheap circle of gold
in place of your narrow wedding band
(your finger felt empty
without it
you said).

it sits like an emblem, a reminder on my windowsill.
you never did finish your degree
—were one credit short.

my mother's hands

i never believed my mother when she said you can tell a lot about a person by their hands. except for the girl i knew in second grade, who had a small purplish scar (the colour of newborn feet) on each hand at the base of her tiniest knuckle where a sixth finger had been amputated. to me hands were just hands. my mother claimed you can tell whether or not to trust someone by their hands. stubby fingers a sure sign of insincerity. spatulate fingertips an index of criminal tendencies. artistic hands, she said, are the most desirable, their delicate skin, attenuated fingers a reflection of superlative thoughts, loftier pursuits. she said a person's hands are as predetermined as the colour of eyes, the set of a jaw. one pair of hands containing all the knowledge, every memory of an entire life.

i remember watching my mother's hands, marvelling at how much she could hold within them. the way she could mend a hole in a torn shirt just by touch, eyes never off the open paperback on her lap, fingers knowing exactly the required number of stitches, brilliant needle squeezing between pinched thumb and index finger from the backside of the fabric, always missing her skin. the way she baked bread from scratch never following a recipe, fingers curved in a delicate scoop, measuring flour into warm water and dissolved yeast until it felt right. the way her hands shaped punched-down dough into white loaves as carefully as folding clean diapers. the way she rapped the hollow-sounding bottom of a loaf like a conjurer casting a spell. and how after brushing butter with her bare fingers on the hot tops of new bread she'd stand back from the counter, one hand dusting flourstreaks down the back of her pants, a salty finger from the other resting on her lower lip.

fallout

the family stories you used to tell; way of holding your body, moving your hands, rhythms of language voicelessly passed from grandmother to mother, mother to you. memory-filled fingers

tugging your black hair like a little girl, you told me of the revulsion you felt for your mother. how you waited for her to give in to the cancer hugging the walls of your sunnyside avenue house. when i recall the sound of your voice,

cracking awkwardly backwards into childhood, i remember you as the 88 pound woman with lymphoma, mother with the pale tennisball stinging the side of her neck, radiated skin crusted brown like overdone toast. i see myself

clinging to a sagging peanutbutter sandwich, standing at the foot of your bed, afraid to move nearer, afraid to touch you, afraid to look you in the eye. the embarrassment

of bringing home friends. i never knew how to explain your blanketed figure on its side in the metal-framed bed, back surrendered against the wall, knees pulled to your chest.

i'd ask if you were okay. you'd answer in a medicated tongue that you were just tired, but i never believed you. how could you be so tired

when all you did was sleep? now i find myself doing the same; lying under cover for three-quarter days, my mind turning around and around like a caught needle. i remember watching your cancersteeped body shrinking

thin-skinned skull sinking into a stack of pillows. i remember my silent disappointment, skulking home to find you still alive.

ghost glowing

remember the summer you carved your hands in a block
of sandstone, fingers branching anxiously, veins
in relief like fossils pushed inside out? you placed this
sculpture under an elm tree in the front yard, porous
stone turning dark and spotted in the rain, texture and
tone changing with the seasons.

i went past the old wood house in the middle of the night,
imagined you moving from room to room, a ghost glowing,
pulling aside walls as easily as curtain sheers.

i forgot to look for the stone, but i could see your hands,
beaten by weather, older, more tenuous than i remember,
fingers gripping sides of trees for balance, nails digging
into bark for dear life.

and what of the dead? i wonder if you can see me, if you
laugh at my transforming your used-up life into poems, if
you ever cry tears stinging of sea-water.

1925, howard street

a man carries a block of ice into the back of a house. the tips of his silver tongs leave subtle impressions on the hardsoft surface of the ice, like forceps on a baby's skull. behind him on the sidewalk up the wooden steps across the kitchen linoleum he trails tiny pools of water. a small girl stands in the corner watching the man. she wonders about the darkness at the centre of the block. it reminds her of her brother holding his hand in front of a candleflame, black bones almost discernible. she knows there is something trapped inside the ice, a small dark animal, a secret winter flower. she'll wait for the block to melt, she does every week, checking the icebox repeatedly, but she'll find only water. such a small girl not fast enough for a creature that lives on cold. as the man stoops to fit the ice in the box he rolls his eyes up knowingly at the girl—for a moment the two are frozen, their eyes transfixed. the block of ice suspended between them.

birthmark

a woman examines a photo of a girl with surgical gauze concealing her face. the girl is standing in a round room in front of a window, light pouring in illuminating the white bandages. she's had a patch of pigment removed from the left side of her face, an orangebrown continent afloat from birth, migrating down her temple, behind her ear, slowly darkening the interior of her cheek. when the bandages are removed there are temporary abrasions on the girl's face, the only traces of her birthmark.

the woman doesn't remember this. the image of the girl is foreign to her. she mentally unravels the bandages from her head, remaps her face with the orangebrown continent. as the woman puzzles over the photograph, her fingers unconsciously explore the left side of her face, tracing the borders of discolouration still floating behind her ear.

a margin of yellow

i remember you painting in the half light
sun edging in around the pulled blind
a margin of yellow all you could stand

that initial stroke always the hardest
fear of botching
creating
nothing at all

this is where we go to escape:
uncertainty of colour
elusiveness
of perception

unburying ruth's ashes

her history seems calcified now
ashes in a plastic bag
brittle with splinters of bone
flakes of marrow.
i rub the gritty powder
between my fingers

taste the salt
the texture of chalk
upon my tongue

i remember the waxy butterboxes of lime
in the crawlspace beneath our house.
with these lumps we'd trace
hopscotch patterns in the backlane
or hide behind their floury explosions
when we'd pelt them
like grenades against
the side of the garage.

i taste the salt
the texture of chalk
upon my tongue

i remember the smell of our shepherd's paws
salty like the soil, salty with earth
as we'd lie on the front porch in the dust
under the sun, the heat making her black pads
swell with the scent of soda crackers
the kind we'd have after school for lunch
dry squares turning spongy in tomato soup, turning it pink.
we'd hold these crackers to the window
watch the sun poke rays through tiny holes.

i taste the salt
and the texture of chalk
upon my tongue

i rub her greyish powder on my arms in streaks
remember the dry egg tempera mixed into fingerpaint—
smell like nothing else—blue and green and magenta
fingerstreaks of trees and animals and birds
slimy liquid transforming
white blank glossiness into
a world oozing between my fingers.

i feel clumps of earth under my knees
two-day-old rain coming through denim
and empty
the plastic bag of its contents
decade-old powder sifting between my fingers.
i knead it with the black earth, like raisins
like chocolate chips into unflavoured dough.

i taste the salt
the texture of chalk
upon my tongue
inhale it like a drug
and remember how
when she died
we said we were ruthless
—wonder if it's so.

as for the living?

we wait

jokes at breakfast

I know
the days of a pig...
are numbered

—Denise Levertov

toetag #1

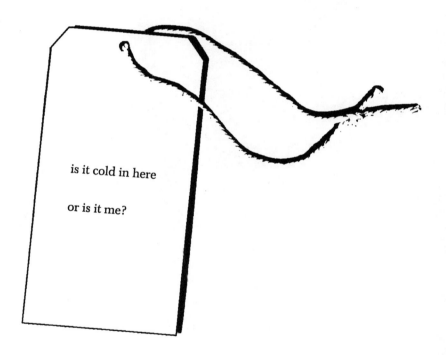

is it cold in here

or is it me?

toetag #2

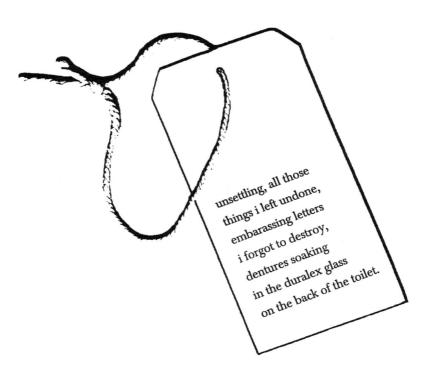

unsettling, all those
things i left undone,
embarassing letters
i forgot to destroy,
dentures soaking
in the duralex glass
on the back of the toilet.

toetag #3

if only you'd give it a chance you'd realize how much we have in common.

for the first time i feel in synch with another body, relaxed here next to me. (too bad we're both flat on our back.)

funny, all those years i dreaded the inevitable. true, i've never experienced a coldness like this, but i have a hunch these refrigerated walls are only the beginning. i feel it in my bones.

toetag #4

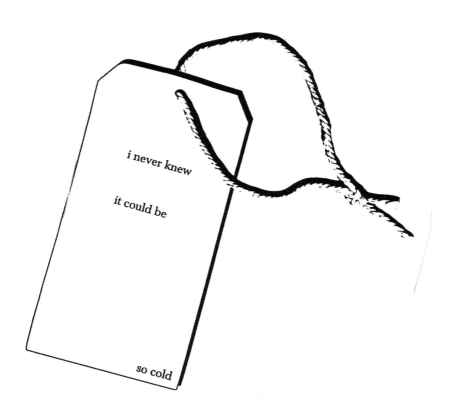

deep snow

i found a book of poems by a man who killed himself unable
to move through deep snow

i've heard it begins in the legs memory starts going
one afternoon you find yourself paralyzed halfway up the front walk
aluminum shovel frozen between shoulder and waist

you forget to plug in the car break two coffee mugs
while you're doing the dishes the storm door bangs back and forth
back and forth

you can't get comfortable in bed untuck retuck ends of
the blanket punch the pillow into various arrangements check
the luminous dial repeatedly

in the morning you cut your hand on broken glass in the sink
can't make coffee because a watermain has burst

the storm door hangs by a single hinge

the car won't start without a boost

insect clocks: one

i dreamed a queen ant, a mother queen ant surrounded by her brood of white larvae spoke to me. i dreamed my mother, buried up to her neck in mothballs translucent as insect eggs, diaphanous as jewels, craned her neck back against her soapwhite pillow, lowered her solid mandible like a hinge, and spoke to me:

>i'm so tired of air perfumed
>
>with napthalene, windows bolted
>
>like a casket. i lie here
>
>in my attic bed, skull slamming
>
>with doors, eyes streaming
>
>white incense. my children don't
>
>know how i wait, buried
>
>under coats of shimmering crystals,
>
>unpacked each morning from the
>
>brass-edged trunk—where i hoard
>
>bits of my life—bearing down
>
>tighter than six feet of earth.

insect clocks: two

startled from a dream. nerve endings bristling up
and down. up. down. arms. legs. ants combing
sun-blanched hair supple as grass. soft. as sand.
i dreamed my mother on an empty beach. the sun
blinding. a queen buried beneath pyramids hot as
anthills. a queen ant in her sand-walled castle.

her steepled fingertips stretch heavenward. collect
grit. seaweed. plaited like hair. strewn like limbs.
an insect praying   a mantis
in supplication.

letter to a pig

dear pig: do you mind that people talk about you
behind your back? discuss your welfare, your future,
your relative plumpness? the brother who tends the
chicken barn at st. peter's told me that pigs are
like god: they love everyone. i don't know about god,
of anything beyond the here and now—i'm not sure
about love. i know what it's like to be near someone
you care for, to smell them beneath your skin, carry
their scent like a memory.

and you, pig, what about you? two weeks of my scratching
your bristly back in the february air, of inhaling the
velvet aroma of your pink ears, sharing your intimate
language of grunts and snorts. could you still love me
knowing i've had bacon for breakfast three days in a
row, pork chops last night, pea soup with ham for lunch?
would you care about me if you knew the truth?

one morning before the sun was up, stillness loud enough
to unnerve a carcass, i saw one of your siblings through
a window in the abbey kitchen. i made jokes at breakfast
about your sister being that evening's menu. did she
have children? parents? a lover? did she trust humans
the way you do? did she nudge poems in the moist earth
with her soft snout?

insect clocks: three

in a dream my mother lounges on a deckchair.
silver hair, sequined skin, one foot tucked
under the other
—motions
with her fin: *here, i'm here.*

i dream my mother. silverfish swimming
backs of my lids, seaweed waving

calming, her moving imperceptibly, breath
on water.

        calling: hear, hear

words

        drown

insect clocks: four

dream opens the same way:
life span
short
as her wings

i am pinning insects: hymen-
optera

skin thin between us

dog day

the dog paces up and down the hallway. the woman who feeds the dog, takes him for walks, lets him sleep on the couch, is passed out on the hardwood floor. the dog sticks his head in and out of the bedroom, each time bringing his nose slightly closer to the woman's body.

every window in the house is shut, both doors locked from the inside. sunlight floods through the open blinds of the bedroom. the rest of the house is dark. when the dog stands half in half out, his body feels confused by the difference in light.

the dog has not been fed since the night before. he needs to urinate badly. the woman has trained him not to go in the house by rubbing his nose in it.

finally the dog moves close enough to nudge the backs of her bare legs with his nose. her skin feels cool against his cold nose, her smell changed.

the dog paces up and down the hallway. dish empty, he wants to be fed.

toetag #5

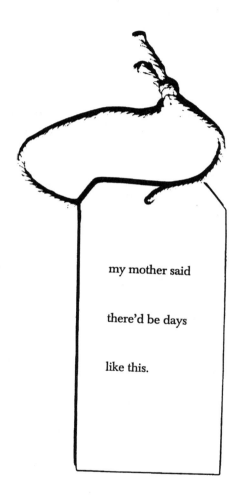

my mother said

there'd be days

like this.

empty screen   (78 lbs)

pornographies

i

a girl punches tickets
out of a cashregister
from behind a window

except for a semi-circular cut
at the base of the glass
she's sealed off
from external contact

she'll work a ten hour shift
damp fingers slipping
in and out all day   like tongues
                                  fingers
seldom touching   exchanging
crumpled five dollar bills
for paper tickets

sometimes the bills are wadded
in tight blue balls
flung at her through the cut

at the end of her shift under
running water she peels open
crumpled bills like scabs

       cum

          streaking

           wilfred laurier's

          blue face

ii

at night she sweeps
sticky condoms
from between seats

never touch

anything

with your bare hands

the projectionist warns her

he's concerned

about safety

iii

the vice cops
wear latex gloves
when they serve hookers
VD warrants

iv

they stop in
during their rounds
for a quick piss
coffee and pop
corn

                    (never wash their hands before

eating)

v

after work she hangs over the toilet bowl

throws up a three hour binge   (length

                                      of a double bill)

started with popcorn

soft corn soft

                  (they always order extra butter
leave flattened tubes of KY jelly

                                            Vaseline
        between rows like

                  corn rhymes with porn

                        always these jokes)

vi

(it'll be years before she can go to a movie   the smell

of popcorn makes her retch)

vii

she knows she's finished

by the yellow bile the

brown husk markers

at the bottom of her stomach–

viii

—a different sort of climax:

with enough practice you don't even need fingers

down the throat
                        simply a matter of muscle

                (she heard a man call his penis
                    his love muscle   only a joke he said
            later she heard he jumped bail
    skipped to the states   out on a rape charge

            skip to my lu my darling)

ix

a matter of muscle

control

x

the projectionist teaches her
35 mm equipment
carbon arc projection

(2 carbons   negative   positive
       create a charge
            power
                  surge on contact)

he trains her well—had his
IATSE card for years—gives her
full benefit of his knowledge

believes in affirmative
action

        (shows her how

               to make 2 carbons fuck)

perfect pitch (notes for my mother)

> *Since you were buried*
> *Your singers are scattered like dust.*
>   —Kuan P'an-p'an (8th-9th century)

*

i write in my brother's house over christmas.
he lives six blocks from the house our mother was born in.
no ghosts except ones i bring.

*

my mother sleeps in a room at the top of stairs.
at night the house breathes
night
hear her breath.

*

houses on sunnyside old as my mother her mother
her mother's mother.
red brick steeped in blood.

*

every time a truck rolls by
the windows of my mother's house shake.
windows of my brother's house shake.

*

someone down the street burns garbage.
my mother watches her brother from the back step empty
ashes from furnace.

*

the man next door rakes leaves between patches of snow.
cigarette lingers on lip
smell of smoke.

*

air in high park so damp my clothes crimp.
my mother's grandmother drapes wet sweaters over radiators.
perfume of wool

*

at the kitchen table in the dark
i sit quietly thinking of you.

*

my mother watches her grandmother making soup.
pinch of salt over shoulder
imperceptible span
between fingers

notes

page 1: the Dorothy Livesay quote is from "Disasters of the Sun," in *The Woman I Am,* Montreal: Guernica, 1991.

page 11: the lines in quotation marks are from "The Warm Left Hand," a poem by Ruth Legris, circa 1971.

page 15: the Susan Griffin quote is from "Hunger," in *Unremembered Country,* Port Townsend: Copper Canyon Press, 1987.

page 35: the Adrienne Rich quote is from "A Woman Dead in Her Forties," in *The Fact of a Doorframe: Poems Selected and New 1950-1984,* New York: W.W. Norton, 1984.

page 46: *and what of the dead* is from "The Truth the Dead Know" by Anne Sexton, in *The Complete Poems,* Boston: Houghton Mifflin, 1981.

page 53: the Denise Levertov quote is from "Her Sadness," in *Pig Dreams: Scenes from the Life of Sylvia,* Woodstock, Vermont: The Countryman Press, 1981.

page 78: the Kuan P'an-p'an epigraph is from "Mourning," in *The Orchid Boat: Women poets of China,* New York: McGraw-Hill, 1972. Edited and translated by Kenneth Rexroth and Ling Chung.

in memory of my mother, ruth evelyn leslie